IF POLAR BEARS DISAPPEARED

To Dad, for instilling in me the power of change

ISBN 978-1-338-64062-5

12 11 10 9 8 7 6 5 4   20 21 22 23 24

Printed in the U.S.A.   40

First Scholastic printing, December 2019

IF POLAR BEARS DISAPPEARED

Lily Williams

SCHOLASTIC INC.

THIS IS THE ARCTIC. It's an ecosystem in the far northern region of the globe. Few animals call this land home. The ones that do live here are

strong,

tough,

slow, and . . .

sometimes hard to see.

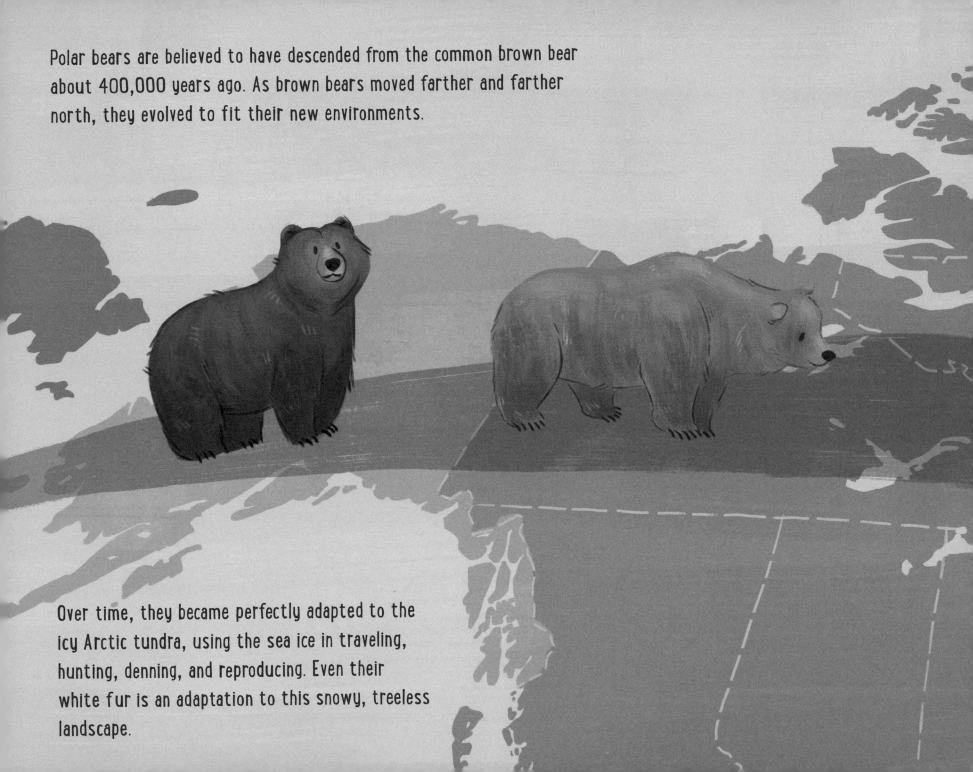

Polar bears are believed to have descended from the common brown bear about 400,000 years ago. As brown bears moved farther and farther north, they evolved to fit their new environments.

Over time, they became perfectly adapted to the icy Arctic tundra, using the sea ice in traveling, hunting, denning, and reproducing. Even their white fur is an adaptation to this snowy, treeless landscape.

Although they're the apex predators in the frozen north, polar bears are still vulnerable to threats like pollution and habitat loss. But the biggest threat to polar bears and other animals in their ecosystem is the melting of sea ice because of climate change.

If too much of the sea ice melted . . .

female polar bears couldn't get enough food to build the layer of fat they need before giving birth to cubs in their dens.

Without enough food, polar bears would be weaker than they should be, and females would have fewer cubs. Some of the cubs wouldn't be healthy enough to survive.

The lack of available food would also cause hungry polar bears to travel outside their natural habitat, forcing them to compete with other predators.

These difficulties would cause the polar bear population to decline, and before long it could dwindle to none.

If too much of the sea ice melted . . .

other Arctic species would be affected as well.

If polar bears become extinct, the number of ringed seals, polar bears' main source of food, could initially rise.

However, because ringed seals also rely on sea ice to mate, fish, rest, and give birth, they would struggle to adapt to the changing environment, too.

If too much of the sea ice melted . . .

ocean predators like orcas would be able to catch more seals, which would cause seal populations to decline even further. With too few seals as prey, orcas could move south, disrupting the balance in the predator—prey relationships in those waters.

If the changes in the Arctic become irreversible, even more species of plants and animals would be affected.

If too much of the sea ice melted . . .

the Arctic north would grow even warmer and the landscape would change permanently.

Shrubs that were once hidden under snow

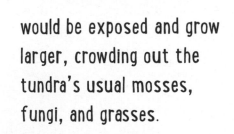

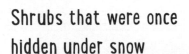

Many of these plant species that are not used to growing in this changing landscape could disappear,

would be exposed and grow larger, crowding out the tundra's usual mosses, fungi, and grasses.

causing herbivores like
caribou to struggle to find
enough food.

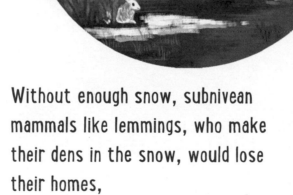

Without enough snow, subnivean
mammals like lemmings, who make
their dens in the snow, would lose
their homes,

exposing them to the harsh
weather and predators, and
decreasing their populations.

SNOWY OWL

ARCTIC GROUND
SQUIRREL

ARCTIC HARE

With many of the herbivores gone, non-apex predators such as the snowy owl and Arctic fox would be the next to lose their main food sources.

Higher temperatures would also alter the reproductive patterns of insects, which in turn could disrupt the migration and breeding patterns of northern birds, who eat insects.

ARCTIC FOX

ERMINE

WILLOW PTARMIGAN

FRESH SNOW

WIND-PACKED CRUST

DENSE SNOW

ICE LENS

DEPTH HOAR

NORTHERN COLLARED LEMMING

Effects like these would begin in the Arctic and spread like a web into different environments.

REFLECTED SUNLIGHT

Snow stays cold because its white color reflects the heat of the sun, sending it back into space. Because bodies of water like the ocean are darker than snow and ice, they absorb the heat of the sun, which warms the water. Then, in a cycle, the warm water causes more sea ice to melt.

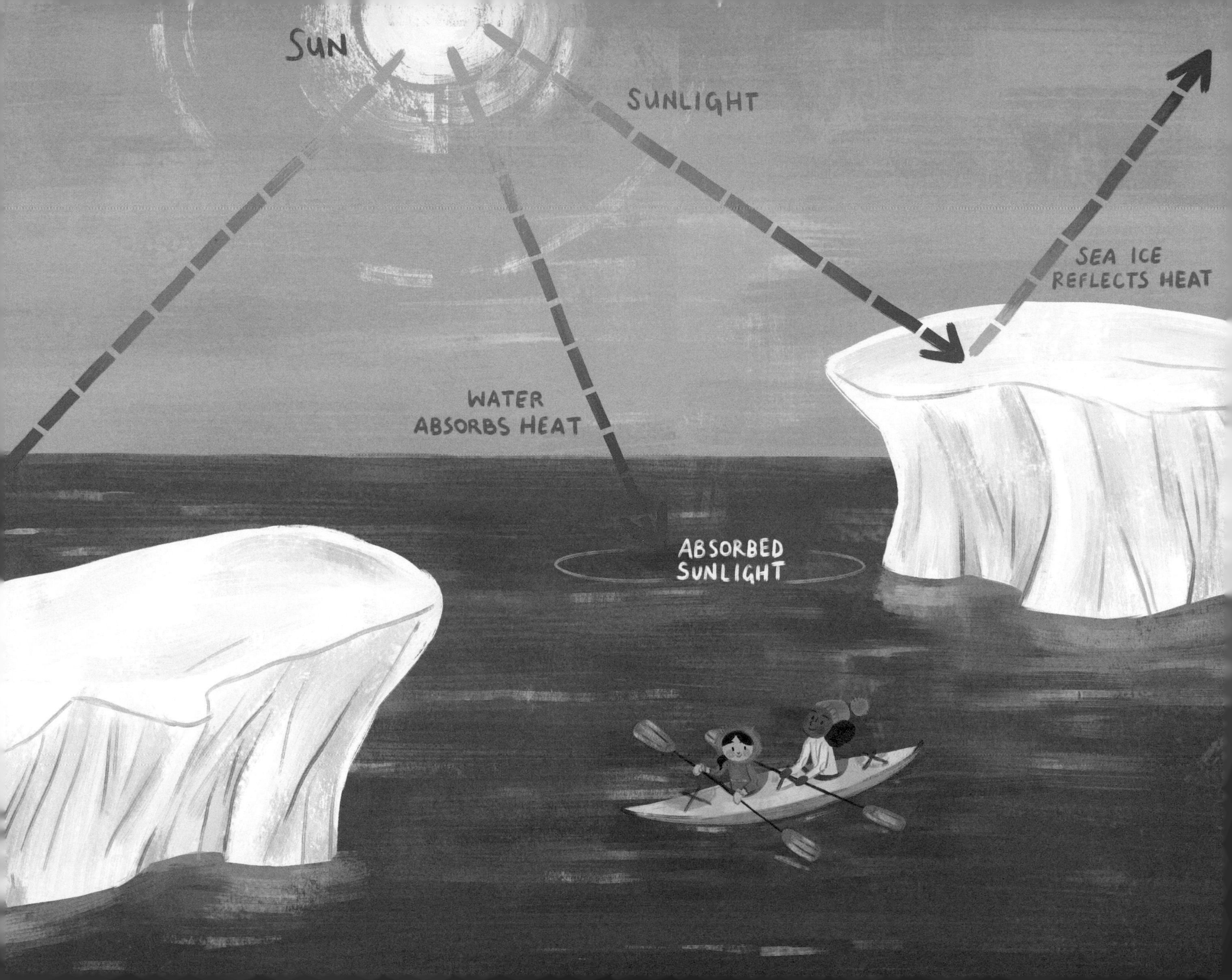

Sun

SUNLIGHT

SEA ICE
REFLECTS HEAT

WATER
ABSORBS HEAT

ABSORBED
SUNLIGHT

This cycle could continue until all the ice has thawed. Then, neighboring ecosystems could change and their animals could disappear. This chain event would roll onward, affecting all the different ecosystems, from the redwood forests, to the hot deserts, to the frozen Arctic, until . . .

we are no longer able to stop it.

Fortunately, we still have time to save polar bears and slow the loss of Arctic ice. Scientists and researchers are working hard to find solutions and educate the public about how ecosystems and organisms are connected to one another.

The best way for you to help is to learn everything you can about climate change and how it affects environments like the Arctic. Taking action will lessen its devastating effects.

And maybe we will find that the answer to saving polar bears . . .

has been right in front of us all along.

GLOSSARY

APEX PREDATOR: the top predator in an ecosystem.

ARCTIC: the region at the top of Earth that is centered around the North Pole and experiences long, cold winters.

ATMOSPHERE: the layers of gases surrounding a planet that are held in place by the planet's gravity.

CLIMATE CHANGE: a marked change in Earth's overall weather patterns or average atmospheric temperatures.

DEN: a cave or secluded area where wild animals live.

DENNING: to live in or inhabit a den.

DEPTH HOAR: big, cup-shaped snow crystals formed at the base of snowpack due to temperature variations.

DESCEND: to originate from a common ancestor.

ECOSYSTEM: a system of living and nonliving things interacting in an environment.

ENVIRONMENT: all the living and nonliving things in a place or region.

EXTINCTION: the deaths, or inability to reproduce, of the last individuals of a species.

GREENHOUSE GAS: a gas that absorbs infrared radiation from the sun, trapping heat and creating a "greenhouse effect" of warming temperatures on Earth. Carbon dioxide, methane, and ozone are examples. The more of these gases there are in the atmosphere, the more heat is trapped.

ICE LENS: a porous, thin layer of ice with cracks that forms as a film atop snow, dirt, or water.

POLLUTION: contamination by an unwanted or harmful substance or thing.

SEA ICE: frozen water on the surface of the ocean. Salt water freezes at 29°F (-2°C).

SUBNIVEAN: a protective zone where the snow meets the ground and where small animals live in winter.

TUNDRA: a cold, treeless landscape with permanently frozen subsoil.

THE ARCTIC IS IN TROUBLE

Our world relies on a delicate equilibrium to stay healthy, and man-made climate change is the largest contributor to a growing imbalance. According to the National Oceanic and Atmospheric Administration, fifteen of the sixteen warmest years on record have occurred since 2001. With temperatures rising consistently, the sea ice in the Arctic is melting at an alarming rate. When too much sea ice is lost, sea levels will rise. This could eventually drown some islands, greatly alter coastlines, and severely impact the fragile Arctic ecosystem. If there's inadequate sea ice, apex predators like polar bears could disappear completely, as could Arctic pinnipeds, including ringed seals.

If less—or no—snow falls, animals such as lemmings and hares that live and are protected within the subnivean ecosystem will be vulnerable to predators, and their numbers will decline. That, in turn, will affect foxes and wolves, which prey on them. Different kinds of ground vegetation could grow as the soil absorbs the warmth of the sun. This could decrease the populations of herbivores like caribou. And without sufficiently cold temperatures in the winter, the Arctic mosquito population could increase so much that they could swarm and prevent the remaining birds and mammals from feeding, starving some and driving others away. The Arctic mosquito is relentless in its pursuit of blood, often causing interruptions in the feeding patterns of caribou.

The challenge posed by climate change in the Arctic is unique because, unlike areas of the world where you can replant trees or fence off plots of land, once the temperature stays above a certain level, sea ice won't refreeze. The higher Earth's temperature rises, the worse the effects of climate change will be, and the more likely the Arctic will be changed forever.

HOW YOU CAN HELP SAVE POLAR BEARS

You can help save the Arctic by making environmentally friendly decisions to help reduce climate change:

• Burn less fossil fuels. Take public transit, bike, walk, or carpool, and be mindful of how much gasoline you use.

• Get your electricity from alternative power sources like solar and wind.

• Turn off lights and unplug other electrical devices when they aren't being used. Make sure the lightbulbs and appliances you do use are energy-efficient.

• Recycle your trash and purchase products that have less packaging. Look to see if you can participate in your community recycling and composting programs.

• Set your home's thermostat lower in the winter and higher in the summer.

• Eat locally produced, sustainable food whenever possible. Check out nearby farmers' markets and food co-ops. Buy products made closer to your home.

• Eat less meat. One pound of beef takes almost two thousand gallons of water to produce, but a pound of vegetables takes much less. Consider adopting meatless Monday.

• Tell your government representatives that you want a renewable energy–based future.

• Encourage people to talk about the environment. Speak out about climate change to spread the word!

AUTHOR'S NOTE

The information in this book is a simplified description of a complex process.
To learn more, start with the Bibliography and Additional Sources listed on the opposite page.

I believe that when art and science are combined, we can create something powerful that inspires learning. The *If . . . Disappeared* books started with sharks in *If Sharks Disappeared*, but now I am traveling the globe to learn about what happens in different ecosystems. Thank you for joining me on my journey!

While some of the information in this book is educated guesses about what might happen, those guesses are based on the best research available from scientists who have studied the Arctic and the rest of the world for many years. I also consulted with Shelby Angalik, a Nunavut, Canada, resident who kindly spent time teaching me about the Inuit people and the realities of life in the icy north. Shelby is an Inuit, the indigenous people of Alaska, northern Canada, and Greenland. In a lot of places around the world, climate change is considered a problem that will arise in the distant future. However, climate change is already a problem for the Inuit because the warmer temperatures and melting ice affect hunting and travel, disrupting their way of life and threatening their deeply held culture.

Climate change is a pressing issue right now, and we can help slow this process. Start by working together to spread facts like the ones in this book. I hope it inspires you to go on a journey yourself, whether it is in search of the truth within the pages of other books, or into the world on a daring adventure. Let's save polar bears—and the planet!

ACKNOWLEDGMENTS

This book would not have been possible without the following people who assisted me in my research and encouraged my exploration: my family, who always believes in my dreams; Minju Chang of BookStop Literary Agency, whose constant support allows me to leap; Emily Feinberg of Roaring Brook Press, without whom none of this would exist; Roberta Pressel of Macmillan, for taking everything to the next level; Nancy Elgin of Macmillan, for her attention to detail; Alysa McCall of Polar Bears International, who advised me with kindness and the cold, hard facts of Arctic science; and Shelby Angalik of Nunavut, who generously shared a glimpse of her world. To them all, I am deeply indebted.

BIBLIOGRAPHY

Angalik, Shelby. Telephone interview, February 9, 2017.

Avingaq, Susan. *Fishing with Grandma*. Illustrated by Maren Vsetula. Iqaluit, Nunavut: Inhabit Media, 2016.

Chester, Sharon. *The Arctic Guide: Wildlife of the Far North*. Princeton, N.J.: Princeton University Press, 2016.

Derocher, Andrew E., Nicholas J. Lunn, and Ian Stirling. "Polar Bears in a Warming Climate." *Integrative and Comparative Biology* 44, no. 2 (2004): 163–176. academic.oup.com/icb/article/44/2/163/674253 /Polar-Bears-in-a-Warming-Climate1.

Hainnu, Rebecca, and Anna Ziegler. *A Walk on the Tundra*. Illustrated by Qin Leng. Iqaluit, Nunavut: Inhabit Media, 2011.

International Union for Conservation of Nature. *Ringed Seals and Climate Change: Arctic Ice Loss Seals the Deal*. IUCN Red List Fact Sheet. Gland, Switzerland: IUCN, 2009. Retrieved September 2016.

Khan, Amina. "Today's Polar Bears All Descended from Single Female Brown Bear, Scientists Say." *The Washington Post*, July 11, 2011.

McCall, Alysa. E-mail interviews, October 2016.

PBS. "The Melting Arctic's Impact on Its Ecosystem." PBS Nature, June 10, 2008. pbs.org/wnet/nature /arctic-bears-the-melting-arctics-impact-on-its-ecosystem/780. Retrieved September 2016.

Pielou, E. C. *A Naturalist's Guide to the Arctic*. Chicago: University of Chicago Press, 1994.

Sulurayok, Matilda. *Kamik's First Sled*. Illustrated by Qin Leng. Iqaluit, Nunavut: Inhabit Media, 2015.

ADDITIONAL SOURCES

Polar Bears International: polarbearsinternational.org

Nunavut Climate Change Center: climatechangenunavut.ca

Alaska Department of Fish and Game: adfg.alaska.gov

LILY WILLIAMS grew up in northern California. She received her B.F.A. with high distinction from California College of the Arts. Lily seeks to inspire change, engage audiences, and educate people of all ages with her artwork. Her work can be seen in films and books and on the web. *If Polar Bears Disappeared* is her second children's book.